Looking at
RUSSIA

Jillian Powell

Gareth Stevens
Publishing

Please visit our web site at: www.garethstevens.com
For a free color catalog describing our list of high-quality books,
call 1-800-542-2595 (USA) or 1-800-387-3178 (Canada).

Library of Congress Cataloging-in-Publication Data

Powell, Jillian.
    Looking at Russia / Jillian Powell.
       p. cm. — (Looking at countries)
    Includes index.
    ISBN-13: 978-0-8368-8173-8 (lib. bdg.)
    ISBN-13: 978-0-8368-8180-6 (softcover)
    1. Russia—Juvenile literature. 2. Russia (Federation)—Social life and customs—
Juvenile literature. I. Title.
DK510.23.P69   2007
947—dc22   2007003490

This North American edition first published in 2008 by
Gareth Stevens Publishing
A Weekly Reader® Company
1 Reader's Digest Road
Pleasantville, NY 10570-7000 USA

This U.S. edition copyright © 2008 by Gareth Stevens, Inc.
Original edition copyright © 2006 by Franklin Watts.
First published in Great Britain in 2006 by Franklin Watts,
338 Euston Road, London NW1 3BH, United Kingdom.

Series editor: Sarah Peutrill
Art director: Jonathan Hair
Design: Storeybooks Ltd.
Picture research: Diana Morris

Gareth Stevens managing editor: Valerie J. Weber
Gareth Stevens editors: Barbara Kiely Miller and Dorothy L. Gibbs
Gareth Stevens art direction: Tammy West
Gareth Stevens graphic designers: Charlie Dahl and Dave Kowalski
Gareth Stevens production: Jessica Yanke

Photo credits: (t=top, b=bottom, l=left, r=right, c=center)
Action Press/Rex Features: 21. AK/Keystone/Rex Features: 15. Heidi Bradner/Panos: 22. Bernd Ducke/Superbild/A1 Pix: 26.
East News/Rex Features: 11. Christiane Eisler/Still Pictures: 19t. Pavel Filatov/Alamy: 7b. Sylvain Grandadam/Robert Harding
PL/Alamy: 13, 23. ©Leslie Richard Jacobs/CORBIS: front cover. Kainulainen/Rex Features: 17t. Jacques Langevin/Sygma/Corbis: 1,
9. Gerd Ludwig/Visum/Panos: 17c. Buddy Mays/Corbis: 18b. Gideon Mendel/Corbis: 12. Mark Newman/Lonely Planet Images: 6.
Oleg Prikhodko: 7t,18t,19b, 20, 27br, 27t. H.Saukkomaa/Rex Features: 16. Sipa Press/Rex Features: 14. Superbild/A1 pix: 4, 8,
10, 25. Superbild/Incolor/A1 pix: 24.

Every effort has been made to trace the copyright holders for the photos used in this book. The publisher apologizes,
in advance, for any unintentional omissions and would be pleased to insert the appropriate acknowledgements in any
subsequent edition of this publication.

Printed in the United States of America

1 2 3 4 5 6 7 8 9 11 10 09 08 07

Contents

Words that appear in the glossary are printed in
boldface type the first time they occur in the text.

Where Is Russia?

Russia is a huge country that lies in both eastern Europe and northern Asia. It is the largest country in the world.

Russia's capital city, Moscow, is in western Russia. Moscow has many large, fancy buildings and **squares**. Many palaces, churches, and statues stand within the walls of the **Kremlin**.

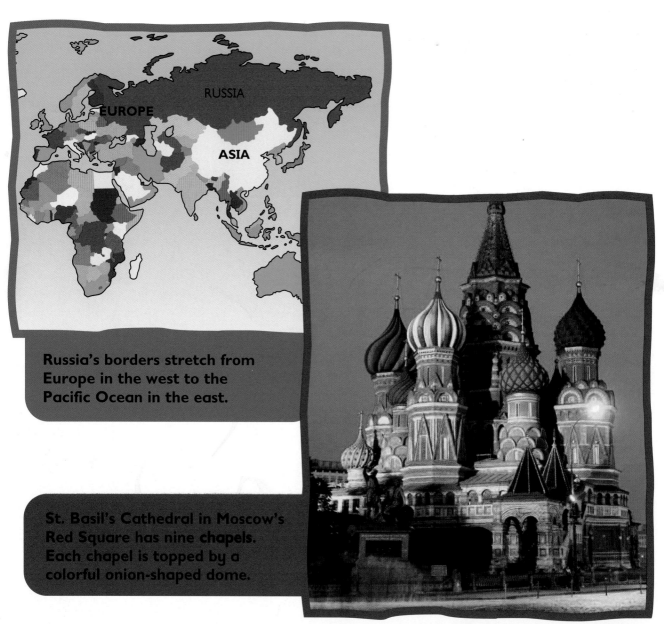

Russia's borders stretch from Europe in the west to the Pacific Ocean in the east.

St. Basil's Cathedral in Moscow's Red Square has nine **chapels**. Each chapel is topped by a colorful onion-shaped dome.

Russia's coastline lies along the Arctic Ocean in the north and along the Pacific Ocean in the east. It shares borders with several countries in Europe and Asia.

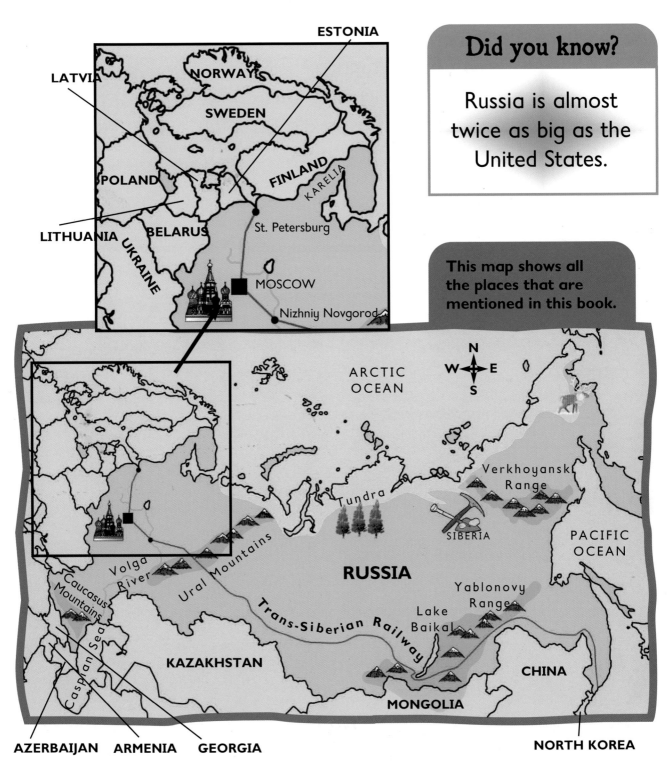

Did you know?

Russia is almost twice as big as the United States.

This map shows all the places that are mentioned in this book.

ESTONIA

NORWAY

LATVIA

SWEDEN

POLAND

FINLAND

KARELIA

St. Petersburg

LITHUANIA

BELARUS

UKRAINE

MOSCOW

Nizhniy Novgorod

ARCTIC OCEAN

N
W E
S

Verkhoyansk Range

Tundra

SIBERIA

PACIFIC OCEAN

Volga River

Caucasus Mountains

Ural Mountains

RUSSIA

Yablonovy Range

Trans-Siberian Railway

Lake Baikal

Caspian Sea

KAZAKHSTAN

CHINA

MONGOLIA

AZERBAIJAN   ARMENIA   GEORGIA

NORTH KOREA

The Landscape

The land farthest north in Russia is tundra. It is a flat landscape without trees, where the soil under the surface is always frozen. South of the tundra, most of northern Russia is a **coniferous** forest called taiga. Central Russia also has huge areas of plains called steppes.

Did you know?

Russia contains nearly one-fourth of the world's woodlands.

Snow and ice melt during the tundra's short summer.

Russia's steppes are covered mainly with grasses and low shrubs.

Russia's highest mountains are the Ural and the Caucasus Mountains. The Ural range runs from north to south and divides European Russia and Asian Russia. The Caucasus Mountains are in the southwest. Russia has some of the world's longest rivers. It also has thousands of lakes, including Lake Baikal, the deepest lake in the world.

This snow-capped peak is in the northern Ural Mountains.

Weather and Seasons

Most of Russia has two main seasons — winter and summer. The winters are long and cold, with lots of snow and ice. The surfaces of rivers and lakes freeze as temperatures fall to −22 °Fahrenheit (−30 °Celsius).

In southern Russia, summers are short and hot. The warmest weather is in July and August. Rain falls mostly during the short spring and early summer months.

Most tourists visit the Summer Palace in St. Petersburg between June and August, during Russia's warmest months.

The Nenets people are reindeer herders. They live along the Arctic coast, one of the coldest parts of Russia.

Northern Russia is cooler than southern Russia. Even the summers are cool along the Arctic coast. A huge area in the north, Siberia has a **subarctic** climate. Temperatures there fall as low as –94 °F (–70°C) in winter.

Did you know?

The snow in Russia is sometimes pink or yellow because of sand and **pollution** in the air.

Russian People

More than 144 million people live in Russia. Most are Russians, but there are more than one hundred other **ethnic groups** including Tatars, Ukrainians, and Chuvash. Each group has its own language, **customs**, **folk dress**, and music. Some live in **republics** that share their government with Russia. Many of the republics would like to be independent nations, however.

Did you know?

Russian babies are often named after **saints**. Children celebrate their "Angel Day" as well as their birthday.

People of the Yakut ethnic group herd cattle and horses in Siberia. This woman is wearing traditional Yakut clothing.

10

These Russian women are celebrating Christmas. They hold religious pictures, called **icons**, that are used when praying.

Most of the people of Russia are Christians, belonging to either the Russian Orthodox or Roman Catholic religions. Russia also has many **Muslims** and Jews.

School and Family

Russian children must start school when they are six years old. Many children with working parents start preschool when they are younger. The school day starts at 8:00 a.m. and finishes at lunchtime for younger children and at 3:00 p.m. for older children. Children can leave school when they are sixteen.

These children are enjoying some playtime outside their school.

This family is using a samovar, a Russian tea urn, to boil water for their tea.

Most Russians have small families with only one or two children. Grandparents often live with the family and help with the housework and childcare.

Country Life

About one-fourth of the Russian people, including the Tatars, the Chuvash, and the Yakut, live in the countryside. In the north, country people herd reindeer, hunt, and fish. In the east, the people herd cattle and horses. In the taiga, many people work in **forestry** or in the timber and paper-making industries.

Russia's cotton crops are picked by hand.

Herbs like these are grown in glass greenhouses. A greenhouse lets in sunlight but protects plants from Russia's cold weather.

The biggest farms are in western Russia. Farmers grow crops, such as wheat and barley, or raise cattle, sheep, or pigs. Sunflower seeds, sugar beets, cotton, and tea are also common crops in Russia. Fruits and vegetables will grow in the warmer south but, in the colder northeast, they must be grown in greenhouses.

Did you know?

Wild hamsters live in Russia's grassy steppes region.

City Life

Most Russian people live in cities. The country's largest cities are Moscow and St. Petersburg.

Both cities have historic buildings and large, open squares alongside tall, modern office and apartment buildings.

When they were built in the 1950s, these buildings near the river in Moscow were the tallest in Europe.

Each year, thousands of people visit St. Catherine's Palace and its gardens in St. Petersburg.

Moscow has government offices, banks, theaters, museums, and busy shops and restaurants. Many streets have kiosks, or stands, selling candy, drinks, cookies, and magazines.

St. Petersburg's main shopping street is often crowded with people.

Many large Russian cities have public transportation, including **trams**, **trolleys**, and trains. People in Moscow, St. Petersburg, and Nizhniy Novgorod also use underground trains to get around.

Russian Houses

Most Russians live in apartment buildings in the **suburbs** of towns and cities. The apartments are usually small. Wealthy families may also own summer homes, or dachas, in the countryside, where they spend vacations.

These apartment buildings, at the front of the photo, are near an industrial area.

Many people grow their own fruits and vegetables at their dachas.

This traditional log house has carvings at the top of its walls and around its windows.

In the countryside, older homes are made of wood. Traditional log houses called *izbas* were built in villages near a church or chapel. Each house has decorations carved around its doors and windows. Many izbas are more than three hundred years old.

Did you know?

In Siberia, some people live in portable tent homes, or yurts.

This colorful carving decorates an izba in the Republic of Karelia.

Russian Food

Traditional Russian dishes include borscht (beetroot soup), *shchee* (cabbage soup), *pelmeni* (a meat-filled pasta dish), and *blini* (thin pancakes). Main meals are usually fish or meat served with potatoes or rice and **pickled** vegetables, such as cabbage or cucumber.

People shop at supermarkets and smaller grocery stores. Special markets also sell fresh foods such as fish and meat.

It is a custom in Russia to greet guests with bread and salt.

The fast-food restaurants in Russian cities are especially popular with young people.

In cities, people eat at Chinese, French, Italian, and Japanese restaurants as well as at those serving traditional Russian dishes. Fast foods such as hamburgers, hot dogs, and ice cream are also popular. Street kiosks sell snacks, including small meat and vegetable pies called *pirozhki* that can be eaten hot or cold.

Did you know?

Russian cooking includes more than one hundred different dishes made from potatoes.

At Work

The main industries in Russia include producing coal, gas, oil, and metals; building ships, aircraft, and machinery; and processing chemicals and foods. Russia also has **textile** and electronics factories.

Siberia is a mineral-rich mining area. This man is working in a **nickel** mine.

This woman is working as a waitress in a restaurant in St. Petersburg.

Most people in Russian cities work in **service industries**, such as banking and insurance. Many people also work in schools, hospitals, restaurants, and hotels.

The tourism industry in Russia is growing fast. City tours, cruises on the Volga River, and trips on the Trans-Siberian Railway are all popular with tourists. Many also like to buy traditional Russian crafts, such as wooden dolls and decorative painted boxes and eggs.

Having Fun

Russians enjoy many sports. In summer, watching soccer is popular. In winter, many people enjoy ice hockey, skating, and snow sports such as skiing. Chess is also popular in Russia, and many people belong to chess clubs. In the cities, people also enjoy going to the ballet and the theater.

Russian ballet dancers perform famous ballets, such as *Swan Lake*, all over the world.

This traditional ring dance is part of a Winter Festival celebration in St. Petersburg.

A Winter Festival is held each year from December 25 to January 5. Russians celebrate with skating, dancing, **troika** rides, and contests for the best ice sculpture.

Did you know?

In Russia, Christmas Day is celebrated on January 7th.

Russia: The Facts

• Russia is a republic. It is made up of many cities, regions, and twenty-one smaller republics.

• Russia is the largest country in the world, with an area of about 6.6 million square miles (17 million square kilometers).

• In Russia, the president is the **head of state** and leads the government. Laws are made by a group called the State Duma.

• Until 1991, Russia was part of the Soviet Union along with fourteen other countries. Some of these countries now form a group of independent nations.

The Russian flag has wide bands of white, blue, and red.

This decorated, dome-topped church is in a small village. Some villages in Russia have as many as thirty churches.

The currency of Russia is the ruble.

Did you know?

Russia has more than one hundred national parks and wildlife reserves. The government looks after these wild areas carefully.

Glossary

chapels – buildings or rooms used for worship

coniferous – describes trees that have needles instead of leaves

customs – ways of doing things that have been passed down for many years

ethnic group – a group of people who have the same national background, language, religion, or culture

folk dress – special kinds of clothing that are passed down for many years in a particular country

forestry – the science and work of growing and caring for trees to be harvested for wood and paper products

head of state – the main representative of a country

icons – religous artworks painted on small, wooden boards

Kremlin – the buildings of the Russian government in Moscow; also a nickname for the Russian government

Muslims – people who believe in the religion of Islam

nickel – a hard, silver-colored metal

pickled – a food kept fresh and flavored by storing it in vinegar

pollution – dirt in the air, on land, or in bodies of water that is caused by waste and chemicals from people and businesses

republics – governments in which decisions are made by the people of a country and their representatives

saints – angels or very good people who have died and are worshipped for their holiness

service industries – businesses that serve people as opposed to businesses that make objects

squares – open, rectangular areas formed where two or more streets meet

subarctic – the kind of climate or landscape found next to the Arctic region

suburbs – areas outside of large cities made up mostly of homes

textile – describes thread, yarn, woven materials, and cloth

trams – bus- or trainlike passenger vehicles that run on rails

troika – a sled for carrying people, pulled by three horses

trolleys – buses powered by electricity

Find Out More

Kids Culture Center: Russia
www.kidsculturecenter.com/russia/russia.htm

Scholastic Global Trek: Welcome to Russia
www.teacher.scholastic.com/activities/globaltrek/destinations/russia.htm

Time for Kids: Russia
www.timeforkids.com/TFK/hh/goplaces/main/0,20344,595847,00.html

Publisher's note to educators and parents: Our editors have carefully reviewed these Web sites to ensure that they are suitable for children. Many Web sites change frequently, however, and we cannot guarantee that a site's future contents will continue to meet our high standards of quality and educational value. Be advised that children should be closely supervised whenever they access the Internet.

My Map of Russia

Photocopy or trace the map on page 31. Then write in the names of the countries, bodies of water, regions, republics, cities, and land areas and mountains listed below. (Look at the map on page 5 if you need help.)

After you have written in the names of all the places, find some crayons and color the map!

Countries
Azerbaijan
Belarus
China
Estonia
Finland
Georgia
Kazakhstan
Latvia
Lithuania
Mongolia
North Korea
Norway
Poland
Russia
Sweden
Ukraine

Bodies of Water
Arctic Ocean
Caspian Sea
Lake Baikal
Pacific Ocean
Volga River

Regions
Siberia

Republics
Karelia

Cities
Moscow
Nizhniy Novgorod
St. Petersburg

Land Areas and Mountains
Caucasus Mountains
Ural Mountains
Tundra
Verkhoyansk Range
Yablonovy Range

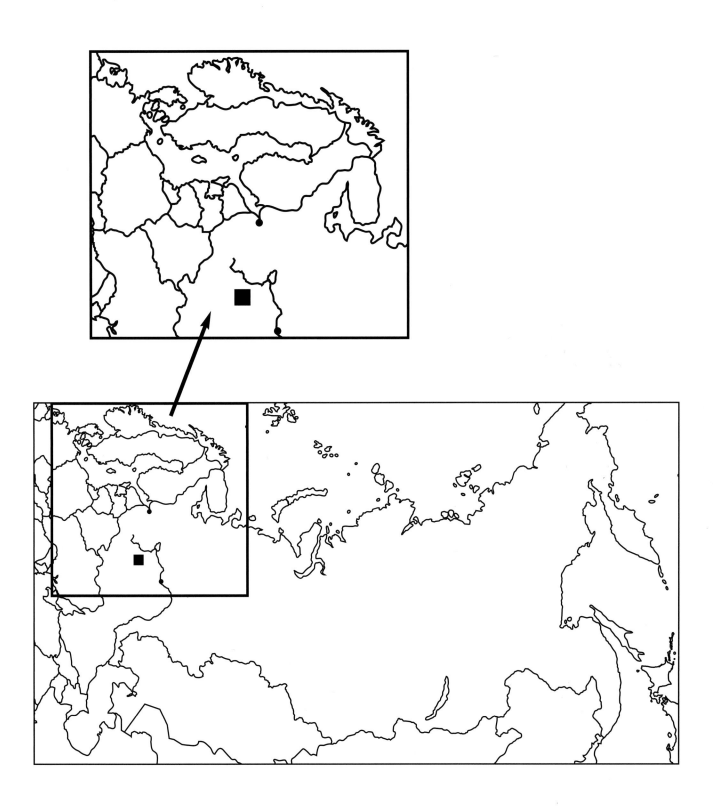

Index